Flag Day

Mir Tamim Ansary

Heinemann Library
Chicago, Illinois

Customer Service 888-454-2279
Visit our website at www.heinemannlibrary.com

Designed by Depke Design
Printed and bound at Lake Book Manufacturing

06 05
10 9 8 7 6 5 4

Library of Congress Cataloging-in-Publication Data
Ansary, Mir Tamim.
  Flag Day / Mir Tamim Ansary.
      p. cm. -- (Holiday histories)
Includes bibliographical references and index.
  ISBN 1-58810-222-X
  1. Flag Day--Juvenile literature. [1. Flag Day. 2. Flags--United
States--History. 3. Holidays.] I. Title.
  JK1761 .A57 2001
  394.263--dc21
                                        2001000072

Acknowledgments
The author and publishers are grateful to the following for permission to reproduce
copyright material:
Cover photograph: Corbis
pp. 4–5, 13 SuperStock; p. 6 Gary Conner/Photo Edit; pp. 7, 10, 11, 17, 27, 28 The Granger
Collection; pp. 8, 14, 19, 20–21 North Wind Pictures; pp. 9, 12, 16, 22, 29 Corbis; p. 15 Historical
Society of Pennsylvania/The Bridgeman Art Library; p. 18 FPG/Getty; pp. 23, 24, 26 Underwood
Photo Archives; p. 25 Culver Pictures.

Every effort has been made to contact copyright holders of any material reproduced in this book.
Any omissions will be rectified in subsequent printings if notice is given to the publisher.

Some words are shown in bold, **like this.** You can find
out what they mean by looking in the glossary.

Contents

Flag Day

June 14 may seem like just another day.
Summer vacation is a few weeks old now.
Most grown-ups have gone to work.

But look around your neighborhood. You
may see more flags than usual. That is
because June 14 is not just another day.
It is Flag Day.

A Promise of Loyalty

On this day our country's flag is flown from many buildings. It is **honored** in our nation's **capital.** People gather to say the Pledge of Allegiance.

People show their loyalty to our country by flying flags during elections, Fourth of July celebrations, and Flag Day.

In the Pledge of Allegiance, people promise their **loyalty** to the flag. But they are not just talking about a piece of cloth. The flag is much more than that.

How Flags
Were Invented

Flags were invented for use in war. Leaders
held them up on crowded battlefields. Soldiers
could then see where their leader was.

A leader's flag came to stand for the leader. Then it came to stand for the leader's land and people. By the 1600s, every country had its own special flag.

Our First Flags

Our country formed after winning a war. We started as thirteen **colonies** controlled by **Great Britain.** We went to war to become a country of our own.

The **colonists** had several flags at first. One looked like the British flag. Another showed a snake over the words "Don't **tread** on me."

Grand Union Flag or Continental Colors, 1775–1777

Continental Navy Flag, 1775

DONT TREAD ON ME

The Stars and Stripes

Then, a man named Francis Hopkinson **designed** a new flag. It had thirteen stars and stripes, one for each **colony.** On June 14, 1777, the **colonists** chose this flag.

Francis Hopkinson

After the war, the colonists formed a new country. But they kept the "Stars and Stripes" as their flag. Each star and each stripe now stood for a state.

★

Changing Country, Changing Flag

But the new country was still growing. Its people were moving west. The **government** was buying or getting more land.

This picture shows a Fourth of July celebration in 1818.
Our country had twenty states then.

New states kept forming. The flag had to
be changed with each new state. One more
star and stripe had to be added.

Back to Thirteen Stripes

By 1818, our country had twenty states. With twenty stripes, the flag looked too crowded. American leaders agreed to one last change.

They decided the flag would always have just thirteen stripes. These would stand for the first thirteen **colonies.** Only a star was added for each new state after that.

The First Flag Day

In 1885, the flag was 108 years old. That year, a teacher in Wisconsin named Bernard Cigrand had an idea. He and his students held a birthday party for the flag.

George Balch's kindergarten class would have looked like this one from the 1880s.

Another teacher named George Balch heard about this party. Balch taught kindergarten in New York City. He had his children celebrate Flag Day, too.

The Flag Day Celebration

On those early Flag Days, students gathered at their schools. Each student was given a small flag.

Then they sang **patriotic** songs. They listened to speeches about their country. They **saluted** the flag as it was raised.

Flag Day Spreads

Balch told the leaders of the New York schools about his flag party. They were in charge of all the schools in New York. They liked what Balch had done.

Schools outside of New York celebrated Flag Day, too.

They asked that all New York schools **observe** Flag Day in 1889. The idea soon spread. In Chicago, 300 thousand children took part in Flag Day in 1894.

★

Flag Day in World War One

In 1916, a **world war** was being fought. Our country was about to join in. President Wilson wanted the country to feel **patriotic**.

He called for a **national** Flag Day that year.
The flag was **honored** across the country.
After the war, people continued to celebrate
Flag Day.

These soldiers celebrate the end of World War Two.
It lasted from 1939-1945.

Flag Day Becomes Official

By 1949, another **world war** had ended. Our soldiers had helped to win this war. Americans felt proud.

President Truman signed a law that said Flag Day should be celebrated every year. Today, it is **observed** in every state. In Pennsylvania it is a holiday.

President Harry Truman

War and Peace

Many people think of soldiers when they see the flag. Soldiers have carried our flag into many battles. But the flag is not just about war.

Explorers, athletes, artists, and scientists have carried our flag, too. On Flag Day, we **honor** our country's strength in peace as well as war.

★

Important Dates

Flag Day

1775	The **colonists** begin their war for independence
1777	Americans choose the Stars and Stripes as their flag
1783	The United States becomes a country
1818	Congress changes the flag back to having thirteen stripes
1877	The flag is one hundred years old
1885	Flag Day is celebrated by Bernard Cigrand and his class
1889	Flag Day is **observed** by the New York schools
1894	300 thousand children celebrate Flag Day in Chicago
1916	President Wilson **declares** a **national** Flag Day
1949	President Truman declares a yearly Flag Day
1960	The last two stars are added to the United States flag

Glossary

capital important city where the government of a country or state is based

colony land owned or controlled by another country

colonists people who live in a colony

declare to state something

design to think, draw, or build something new

government people in charge of a country

Great Britain name that includes England, Scotland, and Wales; people
from Great Britain are called British

honor to show respect for someone or something

loyalty being faithful to; on the side of

national having to do with the whole nation

observe to celebrate

patriotic showing love of one's country

saluted greeted with respect

tread step or walk on

world war war in which many nations fight

More Books to Read

Boyer Binns, Tristan. *The American Flag.* Chicago: Heinemann Library, 2001.

Herman, John. *Red, White, & Blue: The Story of the American Flag.* New York:
Penguin Putnam Books for Young Readers, 1998.

Ryan, Pam Munoz. *The Flag We Love.* Watertown, Mass.: Charlesbridge
Publishing, Inc., 1996.

Index